# POLITICS VS.
# LITERATURE

ORWELL'S **4** ESSAYS

IN THE SAME SERIES

I. *Why I Write*

II. *Politics and the English Language*

III. *The Prevention of Literature*

V. *Shooting an Elephant*

VI. *England Your England*

VII. *Orwell on Reading*

VIII. *Inside the Whale*

# *Politics vs. Literature*

An Examination of
*Gulliver's Travels*

GEORGE ORWELL

RENARD PRESS

**RENARD PRESS LTD**

124 City Road
London EC1V 2NX
United Kingdom
info@renardpress.com
020 8050 2928

www.renardpress.com

*Politics vs. Literature* first published in 1946
This edition first published by Renard Press Ltd in 2021

Edited text © Renard Press Ltd, 2021
Extra Material © Renard Press Ltd, 2021

Cover design by Will Dady
Extra Material edited by Tom Conaghan

Printed on Munken Premium White in the UK by Severn

ISBN: 978-1-913724-32-0

9 8 7 6 5 4 3

Renard Press is proud to be a climate positive publisher, removing more carbon from the air than we emit and planting a small forest. For more information see renardpress.com/eco.

All rights reserved. This publication may not be reproduced, stored in a retrieval system or transmitted, in any form or by any means – electronic, mechanical, photocopying, recording or otherwise – without the prior permission of the publisher.

# CONTENTS

*Politics vs. Literature*     7
  Note on the Text     59
  Notes     60

A Brief Biographical Sketch     62
  of George Orwell

# POLITICS VS.
# LITERATURE

I*N GULLIVER'S TRAVELS* HUMANITY is attacked or criticised from at least three different angles, and the implied character of Gulliver himself necessarily changes somewhat in the process. In Part I he is the typical eighteenth-century voyager, bold, practical and unromantic, his homely outlook skilfully impressed on the reader by the biographical details at the beginning, by his age (he is a man of forty with two children when his adventures start) and by the inventory of the things in his pockets, especially his spectacles, which make several appearances. In Part II he has in general the same character, but at moments when the story demands it he has a tendency to develop into an imbecile who is capable of boasting of 'our noble Country, the Mistress of Arts and Arms, the Scourge of France', etc., etc., and at the same time of betraying every available scandalous fact about the country which he professes to love. In Part III he is much as he was in Part I, though, as he is consorting chiefly with courtiers and men of learning, one has the impression that he has risen in the social scale. In Part IV he conceives a horror of the human race which is not apparent, or only intermittently apparent, in the earlier books, and changes into a sort of unreligious anchorite whose one desire is to live in some desolate spot where he can devote himself to meditating on the goodness of the Houyhnhnms. However, these inconsistencies are forced upon Swift by the fact that Gulliver is there chiefly to provide a contrast. It is necessary, for instance, that he should appear sensible in Part I and at least intermittently silly in Part II because in both books the essential manoeuvre is the same – i.e. to make the human being look ridiculous by imagining him as a creature six inches high. Whenever Gulliver is not acting as a stooge there is a sort of continuity in his character, which comes out especially in his resourcefulness and his observation of physical detail. He is much the same kind of person, with the same prose style, when he bears off the warships of Blefuscu, when he rips open the belly of the monstrous rat and when he sails away upon the ocean in his frail coracle made from the skins of Yahoos. Moreover, it is difficult not to feel that in his shrewder moments Gulliver is simply Swift himself, and there is at least one incident in which Swift seems to be venting his private grievance against contemporary society. It will be remembered that when the Emperor of Lilliput's palace catches fire, Gulliver puts it out by urinating on it. Instead of being congratulated on his presence of mind, he finds that he has committed a capital offence by making water in the precincts of the palace, and

> I was privately assured that the Empress, conceiving the greatest Abhorrence of what I had done, removed to the most distant Side of the Court, firmly resolved that those buildings should never be repaired for her Use; and, in the Presence of her chief Confidents, could not forbear vowing Revenge.

According to Professor G.M. Trevelyan (*England Under Queen Anne*),* part of the reason for Swift's failure to get preferment was that the Queen was scandalised by *A Tale of a Tub* – a pamphlet in which Swift probably felt that he had done a great service to the English Crown, since it scarifies the Dissenters, and still more the Catholics, while leaving the established Church alone. In any case, no one would deny that *Gulliver's Travels* is a rancorous as well as a pessimistic book, and that especially in Parts I and III it often descends into political partisanship of a narrow kind. Pettiness and magnanimity, republicanism and authoritarianism, love of reason and lack of curiosity, are all mixed up in it. The hatred of the human body with which Swift is especially associated is only dominant in Part IV, but somehow this new preoccupation does not come as a surprise. One feels that all these adventures, and all these changes of mood, could have happened to the same person, and the interconnection between Swift's political loyalties and his ultimate despair is one of the most interesting features of the book.

Politically, Swift was one of those people who are driven into a sort of perverse Toryism by the follies of the progressive party of the moment. Part I of *Gulliver's Travels*, ostensibly a satire on human greatness, can be seen, if one looks a little deeper, to be simply an attack on England, on the dominant Whig Party and on the war with France, which – however bad the motives of the Allies may have been – did save Europe from being tyrannised over by a single reactionary power. Swift was not a Jacobite, nor strictly speaking a Tory, and his declared aim in the war was merely a moderate peace treaty and not the outright defeat of England. Nevertheless there is a tinge of quislingism in his attitude, which comes out in the ending of Part I and slightly interferes with the allegory. When Gulliver flees from Lilliput (England) to Blefuscu (France) the assumption that a human being six inches high is inherently contemptible seems to be dropped. Whereas the people of Lilliput have behaved towards Gulliver with the utmost treachery and meanness, those of Blefuscu behave generously and straightforwardly, and indeed this section of the book ends on a different note from the all-round disillusionment of the earlier chapters. Evidently Swift's animus is, in the first place, against *England*. It is 'your Natives' (i.e. Gulliver's fellow countrymen) whom the King of Brobdingnag considers to be 'the most pernicious Race of little odious vermin that Nature ever suffered to crawl upon the surface of the Earth', and the long passage at the end, denouncing colonisation and foreign conquest, is plainly aimed at England, although the contrary is elaborately stated. The Dutch, England's allies and target of one of Swift's most famous pamphlets, are also more or less wantonly attacked in Part III. There is even what sounds like a personal note in the passage in which Gulliver records his satisfaction that the various countries he has discovered cannot be made colonies of the British Crown:

> The *Houyhnhnms*, indeed, appear not to be so well prepared for War, a Science to which they are perfect Strangers,

and especially against missive Weapons. However, supposing myself to be a Minister of State, I could never give my advice for invading them... Imagine twenty thousand of them breaking into the midst of an *European* army, confounding the Ranks, overturning the Carriages, battering the Warriors' Faces into Mummy, by terrible Yerks from their hinder hoofs...

Considering that Swift does not waste words, that phrase, 'battering the warriors' faces into mummy', probably indicates a secret wish to see the invincible armies of the Duke of Marlborough treated in a like manner. There are similar touches elsewhere. Even the country mentioned in Part III, where 'the Bulk of the People consist, in a Manner, wholly of Discoverers, Witnesses, Informers, Accusers, Prosecutors, Evidences, Swearers, together with their several subservient and subaltern Instruments, all under the Colours, the Conduct and Pay of Ministers of State', is called Langdon, which is within one letter of being an anagram of England. (As the early editions of the book contain misprints, it may perhaps have been intended as a complete anagram.) Swift's *physical* repulsion from humanity is certainly real enough, but one has the feeling that his debunking of human grandeur, his diatribes against lords, politicians, court favourites, etc., has mainly a local application and springs from the fact that he belonged to the unsuccessful party. He denounces injustice and oppression, but he gives no evidence of liking democracy. In spite of his enormously greater powers, his implied position is very similar to that of the innumerable silly-clever Conservatives of our own day – people like Sir Alan Herbert, Professor G.M. Young, Lord Elton, the Tory Reform Committee or the long line of Catholic apologists from W.H. Mallock onwards: people who specialise in cracking neat jokes at the expense of whatever is 'modern' and 'progressive', and whose opinions are often all the more extreme because they know that they cannot influence the actual drift of events. After all, such a pamphlet as *An Argument to Prove that the Abolishing of Christianity*,* etc., is very like 'Timothy Shy'* having a bit of clean fun with the Brains Trust, or Father Ronald Knox exposing the errors of Bertrand Russell.* And the ease with which Swift has been forgiven – and forgiven, sometimes, by devout believers – for the blasphemies of *A Tale of a Tub* demonstrates clearly enough the feebleness of religious sentiments as compared with political ones.

However, the reactionary cast of Swift's mind does not show itself chiefly in his political affiliations. The important thing is his attitude towards science, and, more broadly, towards intellectual curiosity. The famous Academy of Lagado, described in Part III of *Gulliver's Travels*, is no doubt a justified satire on most of the so-called scientists of Swift's own day. Significantly, the people at work in it are described as 'Projectors' – that is, people not engaged in disinterested research, but merely on the lookout for gadgets which will save labour and bring in money. But there is no sign – indeed, all through the book there are many signs to the contrary – that 'pure' science would have struck Swift as a worthwhile activity. The more serious kind of scientist has already had a kick in the pants in Part II, when the 'Scholars' patronised by the King of Brobdingnag try to account for Gulliver's small stature:

> After much Debate, they concluded unanimously that I was only *relplum scalcath*, which is interpreted literally, *lusus naturae*,* a Determination exactly agreeable to the modern philosophy of *Europe*, whose Professors, disdaining the old Evasion of *occult causes*, whereby the followers of *Aristotle* endeavoured in vain to disguise

their Ignorance, have invented this wonderful solution of All Difficulties, to the unspeakable Advancement of human Knowledge.

If this stood by itself one might assume that Swift is merely the enemy of *sham* science. In a number of places, however, he goes out of his way to proclaim the uselessness of all learning or speculation not directed towards some practical end:

> The learning of (the Brobdingnagians) is very defective, consisting only in Morality, History, Poetry and Mathematics, wherein they must be allowed to excel. But the last of these is wholly applied to what may be useful in Life, to the improvement of Agriculture and all mechanical Arts so that among us it would be little esteemed. And as to Ideas, Entities, Abstractions and Transcendentals, I could never drive the least Conception into their Heads.

The Houyhnhnms, Swift's ideal beings, are backward even in a mechanical sense. They are unacquainted with metals, have never heard of boats, do not, properly speaking, practise agriculture (we are told that the oats which they live upon 'grow naturally') and appear not to have invented wheels.[1] They have no alphabet, and evidently have not much curiosity about the physical world. They do not believe that any inhabited country exists beside their own, and though they understand the motions of the sun and moon, and the nature of eclipses, 'this is the utmost progress of their *astronomy*'. By contrast, the philosophers of the flying island of Laputa are so continuously absorbed in mathematical speculations that before speaking to them one has to attract their attention by flapping them on the ear

---

[1] Houyhnhnms too old to walk are described as being carried on 'sledges' or in 'a kind of vehicle, drawn like a sledge'. Presumably these had no wheels.

with a bladder. They have catalogued ten thousand fixed stars, have settled the periods of ninety-three comets and have discovered, in advance of the astronomers of Europe, that Mars has two moons – all of which information Swift evidently regards as ridiculous, useless and uninteresting. As one might expect, he believes that the scientist's place, if he has a place, is in the laboratory, and that scientific knowledge has no bearing on political matters:

> What I... thought altogether unaccountable was the strong Disposition I observed in them towards News and Politics, perpetually enquiring into Public Affairs, giving their judgements in Matters of State and passionately disputing every inch of a Party Opinion. I have, indeed, observed the same Disposition among most of the Mathematicians I have known in *Europe*, though I could never discover the least Analogy

between the two Sciences; unless those people suppose that, because the smallest Circle hath as many Degrees as the largest, therefore the Regulation and Management of the World require no more Abilities than the Handling and Turning of a Globe.

Is there not something familiar in that phrase 'I could never discover the least analogy between the two sciences'? It has precisely the note of the popular Catholic apologists who profess to be astonished when a scientist utters an opinion on such questions as the existence of God or the immortality of the soul. The scientist, we are told, is an expert only in one restricted field: why should his opinions be of value in any other? The implication is that theology is just as much an exact science as, for instance, chemistry, and that the priest is also an expert whose conclusions on certain subjects must be accepted. Swift in effect makes the same claim for the politician, but he goes one better in that he will not allow the scientist – either the 'pure' scientist or the ad hoc investigator – to be a useful person in his own line. Even if he had not written Part III of *Gulliver's Travels*, one could infer from the rest of the book that, like Tolstoy and like Blake, he hates the very idea of studying the processes of Nature. The 'Reason' which he so admires in the Houyhnhnms does not primarily mean the power of drawing logical inferences from observed facts. Although he never defines it, it appears in most contexts to mean either common sense – i.e. acceptance of the obvious and contempt for quibbles and abstractions – or absence of passion and superstition. In general he assumes that we know all that we need to know already, and merely use our knowledge incorrectly. Medicine, for instance, is a useless science, because if we lived in a more natural way, there would be no diseases. Swift, however, is not a simple lifer or an admirer of the noble savage. He is in favour of civilisation and the arts of civilisation. Not only does he see the value of good manners, good conversation and even learning of a literary and historical kind, he also sees that agriculture, navigation and architecture need to be studied and could with advantages be improved. But his implied aim is a static, incurious civilisation – the world of his own day, a little cleaner, a little saner, with no radical change and no poking into the unknowable. More than one would expect in anyone so free from accepted fallacies, he reveres the past, especially classical antiquity, and believes that modern man has degenerated sharply during the past hundred years.[2] In the island of sorcerers, where the spirits of the dead can be called up at will:

---

2 The physical decadence which Swift claims to have observed may have been a reality at that date. He attributes it to syphilis, which was a new disease in Europe and may have been more virulent than it is now. Distilled liquors, also, were a novelty in the seventeenth century, and must have led at first to a great increase in drunkenness.

> I desired that the Senate of *Rome* might appear before me in one large chamber, and a modern Representative in Counterview, in another. The first seemed to be an Assembly of Heroes and Demigods, the other a Knot of Pedlars, Pick-pockets, Highwaymen and Bullies.

Although Swift uses this section of Part III to attack the truthfulness of recorded history, his critical spirit deserts him as soon as he is dealing with Greeks and Romans. He remarks, of course, upon the corruption of imperial Rome, but he has an almost unreasoning admiration for some of the leading figures of the ancient world:

> I was struck with profound Veneration at the sight of *Brutus*, and could easily discover the most consummate Virtue, the greatest Intrepidity and Firmness of Mind, the truest Love of his Country and general Benevolence for Mankind

in every Lineament of his Countenance... I had the honour to have much Conversation with *Brutus*, and was told that his Ancestors *Junius, Socrates, Epaminondas, Cato* the younger, *Sir Thomas More* and himself were perpetually together: a *Sextumvirate*, to which all the Ages of the World cannot add a seventh.\*

It will be noticed that of these six people only one is a Christian. This is an important point. If one adds together Swift's pessimism, his reverence for the past, his incuriosity and his horror of the human body, one arrives at an attitude common among religious reactionaries – that is, people who defend an unjust order of society by claiming that this world cannot be substantially improved and only the 'next world' matters. However, Swift shows no sign of having any religious beliefs – at least in any ordinary sense of the words. He does not appear to believe seriously in life after death, and his idea of goodness is bound up with republicanism, love of liberty, courage, 'benevolence' (meaning in effect public spirit), 'reason' and other pagan qualities. This reminds one that there is another strain in Swift, not quite congruous with his disbelief in progress and his general hatred of humanity.

To begin with, he has moments when he is 'constructive' and even 'advanced'. To be occasionally inconsistent is almost a mark of vitality in Utopia books, and Swift sometimes inserts a word of praise into a passage that ought to be purely satirical. Thus, his ideas about the education of the young are fathered on to the Lilliputians, who have much the same views on this subject as the Houyhnhnms. The Lilliputians also have various social and legal institutions (for instance, there are old-age pensions, and people are rewarded for keeping the law as well as punished for breaking it) which Swift would have liked to see prevailing in his own country. In the middle of this passage Swift remembers his satirical intention and adds, 'In relating these and the following Laws, I would only be understood to mean the original Institutions, and not the most scandalous Corruptions into which these people are fallen by the degenerate Nature of Man', but as Lilliput is supposed to represent England, and the laws he is speaking of have never had their parallel in England, it is clear that the impulse to make constructive suggestions has been too much for him. But Swift's greatest contribution to political thought, in the narrower sense of the words, is his attack, especially in Part III, on what would now be called totalitarianism. He has an extraordinarily clear prevision of the spy-haunted 'police state', with its endless heresy-hunts and treason trials, all really designed to neutralise popular discontent by changing it into war hysteria. And one must remember that Swift is here inferring the whole from a quite small part, for the feeble governments of his own day did not give him illustrations ready-made. For example, there is the professor at the School of Political Projectors who 'showed me a large Paper of Instructions for discovering Plots and Conspiracies', and who claimed that one can find people's secret thoughts by examining their excrement:

> Because Men are never so serious, thoughtful and intent, as when they are at Stool, which he found by frequent Experiment: for in such Conjunctures, when he used merely as a trial to consider what was the best Way of murdering the King, his Ordure would have a tincture of Green; but quite different when he thought only of raising an Insurrection or burning the Metropolis.

The professor and his theory are said to have been suggested to Swift by the – from our point of view – not particularly astonishing or disgusting fact that in a recent state trial some letters found in somebody's privy had been put in evidence. Later in the same chapter we seem to be positively in the middle of the Russian purges:

> In the Kingdom of Tribnia, by the Natives called Langdon... the Bulk of the People consist, in a Manner, wholly of Discoverers, Witnesses, Informers, Accusers, Prosecutors, Evidences, Swearers... It is first agreed, and settled among them, what suspected Persons shall be accused of a Plot: Then, effectual Care is taken to secure all their Letters and Papers, and put the Owners in Chains. These papers are delivered to a Sett of Artists, very dexterous in finding out the mysterious Meanings of Words, Syllables and Letters... Where this method fails, they have two others more effectual, which the Learned

among them call *acrostics* and *anagrams*. *First*, they can decipher all initial Letters into political Meanings: Thus: N shall signify a Plot, B a Regiment of Horse, L a Fleet at Sea: Or, *secondly*, by transposing the Letters of the Alphabet in any suspected Paper, they can lay open the deepest Designs of a discontented Party. So, for Example, if I should say in a Letter to a Friend, *our brother Tom has just got the piles*, a skilful Decipherer would discover that the same Letters which compose that Sentence may be analysed in the following Words: *Resist – a plot is brought home the tour* (Note: tower). And this is the anagrammatic method.

Other professors at the same school invent simplified languages, write books by machinery, educate their pupils by inscribing the lesson on a wafer and causing them to swallow it, or propose to abolish individuality altogether by cutting off part of the brain of one man and grafting it on to the head of another. There is something queerly familiar in the atmosphere of these chapters because, mixed up with much fooling, there is a perception that one of the aims of totalitarianism is not merely to make sure that people will think the right thoughts, but actually to make them *less conscious*. Then, again, Swift's account of the leader who is usually to be found ruling over a tribe of Yahoos, and of the 'favourite' who acts first as a dirty-worker and later as a scapegoat, fits remarkably well into the pattern of our own times. But are we to infer from all this that Swift was first and foremost an enemy of tyranny and a champion of the free intelligence? No: his own views, so far as one can discern them, are not markedly liberal. No doubt he hates lords, kings, bishops, generals, ladies of fashion, orders, titles and flummery generally, but he does not seem to think better of the common people than of their rulers, or to be in favour of increased social equality, or to be enthusiastic about representative institutions. The Houyhnhnms are organised upon a sort of caste system which is racial in character, the horses which do the menial work being of different colours from their masters and not interbreeding with them. The educational system which Swift admires in the Lilliputians takes hereditary class distinctions for granted, and the children of the poorest classes do not go to school, because 'their Business being only to till and cultivate the Earth... therefore their Education is of little Consequence to the Public'. Nor does he seem to have been strongly in favour of freedom of speech and the Press, in spite of the toleration which his own writings enjoyed. The King of Brobdingnag is astonished at the multiplicity of religious and political sects in England, and considers that those who hold 'opinions prejudicial to the public' (in the context this seems to mean simply heretical opinions), though they need not be obliged to change them, ought to be obliged to conceal them: for 'as it was Tyranny in any Government to require the first, so it was weakness not to enforce the second'. There is a subtler indication of Swift's own attitude in the manner in which Gulliver leaves the land of the Houyhnhnms. Intermittently, at least. Swift was a kind of anarchist, and Part IV of *Gulliver's Travels* is a picture of an anarchistic society, not governed by law in the ordinary sense, but by the dictates of 'Reason', which are voluntarily accepted by everyone. The General Assembly of the Houyhnhnms 'exhorts' Gulliver's master to get rid of him, and his neighbours put pressure on him to make him comply. Two reasons are given. One is that the presence of this unusual Yahoo may unsettle the rest of the tribe, and the other is that a friendly relationship between a

Houyhnhnm and a Yahoo is 'not agreeable to Reason or Nature, or a Thing ever heard of before among them'. Gulliver's master is somewhat unwilling to obey, but the 'exhortation' (a Houyhnhnm, we are told, is never *compelled* to do anything, he is merely 'exhorted' or 'advised') cannot be disregarded. This illustrates very well the totalitarian tendency which is explicit in the anarchist or pacifist vision of Society. In a society in which there is no law, and in theory no compulsion, the only arbiter of behaviour is public opinion. But public opinion, because of the tremendous urge to conformity in gregarious animals, is less tolerant than any system of law. When human beings are governed by 'thou shalt not', the individual can practise a certain amount of eccentricity: when they are supposedly governed by 'love' or 'reason', he is under continuous pressure to make him behave and think in exactly the same way as everyone else.

The Houyhnhnms, we are told, were unanimous on almost all subjects. The only question they ever *discussed* was how to deal with the Yahoos. Otherwise there was no room for disagreement among them, because the truth is always either self-evident, or else it is undiscoverable and unimportant. They had apparently no word for 'opinion' in their language, and in their conversations there was no 'difference of sentiments'. They had reached, in fact, the highest stage of totalitarian organisation — the stage when conformity has become so general that there is no need for a police force. Swift approves of this kind of thing because among his many gifts neither curiosity nor good nature was included. Disagreement would always seem to him sheer perversity. 'Reason,' among the Houyhnhnms, he says, 'is not a Point Problematical, as with us, where men can argue with Plausibility on both Sides of a Question; but strikes you with immediate

Conviction; as it must needs do, where it is not mingled, obscured or discoloured by Passion and Interest.' In other words, we know everything already, so why should dissident opinions be tolerated? The totalitarian society of the Houyhnhnms, where there can be no freedom and no development, follows naturally from this.

We are right to think of Swift as a rebel and iconoclast, but except in certain secondary matters, such as his insistence that women should receive the same education as men, he cannot be labelled 'Left'. He is a Tory anarchist, despising authority while disbelieving in liberty, and preserving the aristocratic outlook while seeing clearly that the existing aristocracy is degenerate and contemptible. When Swift utters one of his characteristic diatribes against the rich and powerful, one must probably, as I said earlier, write off something for the fact that he himself belonged to the less successful party and was personally disappointed. The 'outs', for obvious reasons, are always more radical than the 'ins'.[3] But the most essential thing in Swift is his inability to believe that life – ordinary life on the solid earth, and not some rationalised, deodorised version of it – could be made worth living. Of course, no honest person claims that happiness is *now* a normal condition among adult human beings; but

---

[3] At the end of the book, as typical specimens of human folly and viciousness, Swift names 'a Lawyer, a Pickpocket, a Colonel, a Fool, a Lord, a Gamester, a Politician, a Whore-master, a Physician, an Evidence, a Suborner, an Attorney, a Traitor, or the like'. One sees here the irresponsible violence of the powerless. The list lumps together those who break the conventional code, and those who keep it. For instance, if you automatically condemn a colonel, as such, on what grounds do you condemn a traitor? Or again, if you want to suppress pickpockets, you must have laws, which means that you must have lawyers. But the whole closing passage, in which the hatred is so authentic, and the reason given for it so inadequate, is somehow unconvincing. One has the feeling that personal animosity is at work.

perhaps it *could* be made normal, and it is upon this question that all serious political controversy really turns. Swift has much in common – more, I believe, than has been noticed – with Tolstoy, another disbeliever in the possibility of happiness. In both men you have the same anarchistic outlook covering an authoritarian cast of mind; in both a similar hostility to science, the same impatience with opponents, the same inability to see the importance of any question not interesting to themselves; and in both cases a sort of horror of the actual process of life, though in Tolstoy's case it was arrived at later and in a different way. The sexual unhappiness of the two men was not of the same kind, but there was this in common: that in both of them a sincere loathing was mixed up with a morbid fascination. Tolstoy was a reformed rake who ended by preaching complete celibacy, while continuing to practise the opposite into extreme old age. Swift was presumably impotent, and had an exaggerated horror of human dung: he also thought about it incessantly, as is evident throughout his works. Such people are not likely to enjoy even the small amount of happiness that falls to most human beings, and, from obvious motives, are not likely to admit that earthly life is capable of much improvement. Their incuriosity, and hence their intolerance, spring from the same root.

Swift's disgust, rancour and pessimism would make sense against the background of a 'next world' to which this one is the prelude. As he does not appear to believe seriously in any such thing, it becomes necessary to construct a paradise supposedly existing on the surface of the earth, but something quite different from anything we know, with all that he disapproves of – lies, folly, change, enthusiasm, pleasure, love and dirt – eliminated from it. As his ideal being he chooses the horse, an animal whose excrement is not offensive. The

Houyhnhnms are dreary beasts – this is so generally admitted that the point is not worth labouring. Swift's genius can make them credible, but there can have been very few readers in whom they have excited any feeling beyond dislike. And this is not from wounded vanity at seeing animals preferred to men; for, of the two, the Houyhnhnms are much liker to human beings than are the Yahoos, and Gulliver's horror of the Yahoos, together with his recognition that they are the same kind of creature as himself, contains a logical absurdity. This horror comes upon him at his very first sight of them. 'I never beheld,' he says, 'in all my Travels, so disagreeable an Animal, nor one against which I naturally conceived so strong an Antipathy.' But in comparison with what are the Yahoos disgusting? Not with the Houyhnhnms, because at this time Gulliver has not seen a Houyhnhnm. It can only be in comparison with himself, i.e. with a human being. Later, however, we are to be told that the Yahoos *are* human beings, and human society becomes insupportable to Gulliver because all men are Yahoos. In that case, why did he not conceive his disgust of humanity earlier? In effect we are told that the Yahoos are fantastically different from men, and yet are the same. Swift has overreached himself in his fury, and is shouting at his fellow creatures, 'You are filthier than you are!' However, it is impossible to feel much sympathy with the Yahoos, and it is not because they oppress the Yahoos that the Houyhnhnms are unattractive. They are unattractive because the 'Reason' by which they are governed is really a desire for death. They are exempt from love, friendship, curiosity, fear, sorrow and – except in their feelings towards the Yahoos, who occupy rather the same place in their community as the Jews in Nazi Germany – anger and hatred. 'They have no Fondness for their Colts or Foals, but the Care they take in educating them proceeds entirely from the Dictates of *reason*.' They lay store by 'Friendship' and 'Benevolence', but 'these are not confined to particular Objects, but universal to the whole Race'. They also value conversation, but in their conversations there are no differences of opinion, and 'nothing passed but what was useful, expressed in the fewest and most significant Words'. They practise strict birth control, each couple producing two offspring and thereafter abstaining from sexual intercourse. Their marriages are arranged for them by their elders, on eugenic principles, and their language contains no word for 'love' in the sexual sense. When somebody dies they carry on exactly as before, without feeling any grief. It will be seen that their aim is to be as like a corpse as is possible while retaining physical life. One or two of their characteristics, it is true, do not seem to be strictly 'reasonable' in their own usage of the word. Thus, they place a great value not only on physical hardihood but on athleticism, and they are devoted to poetry. But these exceptions may be less arbitrary than they seem. Swift probably emphasises the physical strength of the Houyhnhnms in order to make clear that they could never be conquered by the hated human race, while a taste for poetry may figure among their qualities because poetry appeared to Swift as the antithesis of science, from his point of view the most useless of all pursuits. In Part III he names 'Imagination, Fancy and Invention' as desirable faculties in which the Laputan mathematicians (in spite of their love of music) were wholly lacking. One must remember that although Swift was an admirable writer of comic verse, the kind of poetry he thought valuable would probably be didactic poetry. The poetry of the Houyhnhnms, he says,

> must be allowed to excel (that of) all other Mortals; wherein the Justness of their Similes, and the Minuteness, as

> well as exactness, of their Descriptions, are, indeed, inimitable. Their Verses abound very much in both of these; and usually contain either some exalted Notions of Friendship and Benevolence, or the Praises of those who were Victors in Races, and other bodily Exercises.

Alas, not even the genius of Swift was equal to producing a specimen by which we could judge the poetry of the Houyhnhnms. But it sounds as though it were chilly stuff (in heroic couplets, presumably), and not seriously in conflict with the principles of 'Reason'.

Happiness is notoriously difficult to describe, and pictures of a just and well-ordered society are seldom either attractive or convincing. Most creators of 'favourable' Utopias, however, are concerned to show what life could be like if it were lived more fully. Swift advocates a simple refusal of life, justifying this by the claim that 'Reason' consists in thwarting your instincts. The Houyhnhnms, creatures without a history, continue for generation after generation to live prudently, maintaining their population at exactly the same level, avoiding all passion, suffering from no diseases, meeting death indifferently, training up their young in the same principles – and all for what? In order that the same process may continue indefinitely. The notions that life here and now is worth living, or that it could be made worth living, or that it must be sacrificed for some future good, are all absent. The dreary world of the Houyhnhnms was about as good a Utopia as Swift could construct, granting that he neither believed in a 'next world' nor could get any pleasure out of certain normal activities. But it is not really set up as something desirable in itself, but as the justification for another attack on humanity. The aim, as usual, is to humiliate man by reminding him that he is weak and ridiculous, and above all that he stinks; and the ultimate motive, probably, is a kind of envy – the envy of the ghost for the living, of the man who knows he cannot be happy for the others who – so he fears – may be a little happier than himself. The political expression of such an outlook must be either reactionary or nihilistic, because the person who holds it will want to prevent society from developing in some direction in which his pessimism may be cheated. One can do this either by blowing everything to pieces, or by averting social change. Swift ultimately blew everything to pieces in the only way that was feasible before the atomic bomb – that is, he went mad – but, as I have tried to show, his political aims were, on the whole, reactionary ones.

From what I have written it may have seemed that I am *against* Swift, and that my object is to refute him, and even to belittle him. In a political and moral sense I am against him, so far as I understand him. Yet curiously enough he is one of the writers I admire with least reserve, and *Gulliver's Travels*, in particular, is a book which it seems impossible for me to grow tired of. I read it first when I was eight – one day short of eight, to be exact, for I stole and furtively read the copy which was to be given me next day on my eighth birthday – and I have certainly not read it less than half a dozen times since. Its fascination seems inexhaustible. If I had to make a list of six books which were to be preserved when all others were destroyed, I would certainly put *Gulliver's Travels* among them. This raises the question: what is the relationship between agreement with a writer's opinions and enjoyment of his work?

If one is capable of intellectual detachment, one can *perceive* merit in a writer whom one deeply disagrees with, but *enjoyment* is a different matter. Supposing that there is such a thing as good or bad art, then the goodness or badness must reside in the work of art itself – not independently of the observer, indeed, but independently of the mood of the observer. In one sense, therefore, it cannot be true that a poem is good on Monday and bad on Tuesday. But if one judges the poem by the appreciation it arouses then it can certainly be true, because appreciation, or enjoyment, is a subjective condition which cannot be commanded. For a great deal of his waking life, even the most cultivated person has no aesthetic feelings whatever, and the power to have aesthetic feelings is very easily destroyed. When you are frightened or hungry, or are suffering from toothache or sea-sickness, *King Lear* is no better from your point of view than *Peter Pan*. You may know in an intellectual sense that it is better, but that is simply a fact which you remember: you will not *feel* the merit of *King Lear* until you are normal again. And aesthetic judgement can be upset just as disastrously – more disastrously, because the cause is less readily recognised – by political or moral disagreement. If a book angers, wounds or alarms you then you will not enjoy it, whatever its merits may be. If it seems to you a really pernicious book, likely to influence other people in some undesirable way, then you will probably construct an aesthetic theory to show that it *has* no merits. Current literary criticism consists quite largely of this kind of dodging to and fro between two sets of standards. And yet the opposite process can also happen: enjoyment can overwhelm disapproval, even though one clearly recognises that one is enjoying something inimical. Swift, whose worldview is so peculiarly unacceptable, but who is nevertheless an extremely popular writer, is a good instance of this. Why is it that we don't mind being called Yahoos, although firmly convinced that we are *not* Yahoos?

It is not enough to make the usual answer that of course Swift was wrong, in fact he was insane, but he was 'a good writer'. It is true that the literary quality of a book is to some small extent separable from its subject matter. Some people have a native gift for using words, as some people have a naturally 'good eye' at games. It is largely a question of timing and of instinctively knowing how much emphasis to use. As an example near at hand, look back at the passage I quoted earlier, starting 'In the Kingdom of Tribnia, by the Natives called Langdon' (p. 31). It derives much of its force from the final sentence: 'And this is the anagram-made Method.' Strictly speaking this sentence is unnecessary, for we have already seen the anagram deciphered, but the mock-solemn repetition, in which one seems to hear Swift's own voice uttering the words, drives home the idiocy of the activities described, like the final tap to a nail. But not all the power and simplicity of Swift's prose, nor the imaginative effort that has been able to make not one but a whole series of impossible worlds more credible than the majority of history books – none of this would enable us to enjoy Swift if his worldview were truly wounding or shocking. Millions of people, in many countries, must have enjoyed *Gulliver's Travels* while more or less seeing its anti-human implications; and even the child who accepts Parts I and II as a simple story gets a sense of absurdity from thinking of human beings six inches high. The explanation must be that Swift's worldview is felt to be *not* altogether false – or it would probably be more accurate to say, not false all the time. Swift is a diseased writer. He remains permanently in a depressed mood which in most people is only intermittent, rather as though someone suffering from jaundice or the after-effects of influenza should have the energy to write books. But we all know that mood, and something in us responds to the expression of it. Take, for instance, one of his most characteristic works, 'The

Lady's Dressing Room': one might add the kindred poem, 'Upon a Beautiful Young Nymph Going to Bed'. Which is truer – the viewpoint expressed in these poems, or the viewpoint implied in Blake's phrase, 'The naked female human form divine'? No doubt Blake is nearer the truth, and yet who can fail to feel a sort of pleasure in seeing that fraud, feminine delicacy, exploded for once? Swift falsifies his picture of the world by refusing to see anything in human life except dirt, folly and wickedness, but the part which he abstracts from the whole does exist, and it is something which we all know about while shrinking from mentioning it. Part of our minds – in any normal person it is the dominant part – believes that man is a noble animal and life is worth living; but there is also a sort of inner self which at least intermittently stands aghast at the horror of existence. In the queerest way, pleasure and disgust are linked together. The human body is beautiful; it is also repulsive and ridiculous, a fact which can be verified at any swimming pool. The sexual organs are objects of desire and also of loathing, so much so that in many languages, if not in all languages, their names are used as words of abuse. Meat is delicious, but a butcher's shop makes one feel sick; and indeed all our food springs ultimately from dung and dead bodies – the two things which of all others seem to us the most horrible. A child, when it is past the infantile stage but still looking at the world with fresh eyes, is moved by horror almost as often as by wonder – horror of snot and spittle, of the dogs' excrement on the pavement, the dying toad full of maggots, the sweaty smell of grown-ups, the hideousness of old men, with their bald heads and bulbous noses. In his endless harping on disease, dirt and deformity, Swift is not actually inventing anything, he is merely leaving something out. Human behaviour, too, especially in politics, is as he describes it, although it contains other more important factors which he refuses to admit. So far as we can see, both horror and pain are necessary to the continuance of life on this planet, and it is therefore open to pessimists like Swift to say: 'If horror and pain must always be with us, how can life be significantly improved?' His attitude is in effect the Christian attitude, minus the bribe of a 'next world' – which, however, probably has less hold upon the minds of believers than the conviction that this world is a vale of tears and the grave is a place of rest. It is, I am certain, a wrong attitude, and one which could have harmful effects upon behaviour; but something in us responds to it, as it responds to the gloomy words of the burial service and the sweetish smell of corpses in a country church.

It is often argued – at least by people who admit the importance of subject matter – that a book cannot be 'good' if it expresses a palpably false view of life. We are told that in our own age, for instance, any book that has genuine literary merit will also be more or less 'progressive' in tendency. This ignores the fact that throughout history a similar struggle between progress and reaction has been raging, and that the best books of any one age have always been written from several different viewpoints, some of them palpably more false than others. In so far as a writer is a propagandist, the most one can ask of him is that he shall genuinely believe in what he is saying, and that it shall not be something blazingly silly. Today, for example, one can imagine a good book being written by a Catholic, a Communist, a Fascist, pacifist, an anarchist, perhaps by an old-style Liberal or an ordinary Conservative; one cannot imagine a good book being written by a spiritualist, a Buchmanite or a member of the Ku-Klux-Klan. The views that a writer holds must be compatible with sanity, in the medical sense, and with the power of continuous thought: beyond that what we ask of him is talent, which is probably another name for conviction. Swift did not possess ordinary wisdom, but he did possess a terrible intensity of vision, capable of picking out a single hidden truth and then magnifying it and distorting it. The durability of *Gulliver's Travels* goes to show that, if the force of belief is behind it, a worldview which only just passes the test of sanity is sufficient to produce a great work of art.

GEORGE ORWELL

1946

# NOTE ON THE TEXT

*Politics vs. Literature: An Examination of Gulliver's Travels* was first published in the September 1946 edition of *Polemic*, which described itself as a 'Magazine of Philosophy, Psychology and Aesthetics'. The text of this edition is based on that of the first publication – although the essay has been republished several times since its initial appearance, no material changes were made in the author's lifetime, and this is still considered the authoritative text. In some instances, spelling, punctuation and grammar have been silently corrected to make the text more appealing to the modern reader, although the italicisation and capitalisation in quotations from Swift's texts have been retained, to preserve Orwell's view of the texts. The footnotes in the text are Orwell's own.

# NOTES

*12* *Professor G.M.... Queen Anne*: A reference to *England Under Queen Anne* (1930–34) by the British historian and academic G.M. Trevelyan (1876–1962).

*18* *An Argument... Christianity*: A reference to a 1708 satirical essay by Swift (properly titled *An Argument to Prove that the Abolishing of Christianity in England May, as Things Now Stand Today, be Attended with Some Inconveniences, and Perhaps not Produce Those Many Good Effects Proposed Thereby*).

*18* *Timothy Shy... Bertrand Russell*: The references are to the writer D.B. Wyndham Lewis (1891–1969), whose sometimes used the nom de plume 'Timothy Shy', the BBC radio programme that aired in the 1940s–50s, where a panel of experts answered audience questions, Ronald Arbuthnott Knox (1888–1957), a Catholic priest and writer, and the polymath Bertrand Russell (1872–1970).

## EXTRA MATERIAL

19 *lusus naturae*: 'Freak of nature' (Latin).

27 *Brutus… cannot add a seventh*: The references are to the Roman general Marcus Junius Brutus (85 BC–42 BC), the founder of the Roman republic, Lucius Junius Brutus (d. *c.*509 BC), the philosopher Socrates (*c.*470–399 BC), the Greek general Epaminondas (418–362 BC), the Roman senator Cato the younger (95 BC–46 BC) and the Catholic saint Sir Thomas More (1478–1535).

# *A Brief Biographical Sketch of George Orwell*

Born Eric Arthur Blair on the 25th of June 1903 in eastern India, George Orwell was a prolific and acclaimed writer, who is chiefly remembered for his politically charged novels – in particular *Animal Farm* and *Nineteen Eighty-Four* – and his longer non-fiction, especially *The Road to Wigan Pier* and *Down and Out in Paris and London*.

In the 1930s, Orwell's political stance became more marked, and in 1936 he travelled to Spain to fight for the Republicans against General Franco. Here, on the 20th of May 1937, he was shot through the throat by a sniper, only narrowly surviving.

In 1941 he took up a position with the BBC, where he produced propaganda.

He departed in 1943 to take up the editorship of *The Tribune*.

With the publication of *Animal Farm* in 1945, Orwell shot to fame, and the financial stability this provided allowed him to devote more of his time to writing than ever before.

In 1947, he was diagnosed with tuberculosis and his health declined until he died, aged 46, on the 21st of January 1950.

Orwell's legacy is astounding – his essays are almost innumerable and his novels have been studied and adored by generations. Orwell devoted his life to working against extremism, and, in his description of how authoritarian regimes pervade our thoughts, he gave us a new vocabulary with which to understand totalitarianism.

## OTHER CLASSIC NON-FICTION FROM RENARD PRESS

ISBN: 9781913724306
60pp • Paperback • £5

ISBN: 9781913724290
48pp • Paperback • £5

ISBN: 9781913724313
64pp • Paperback • £5

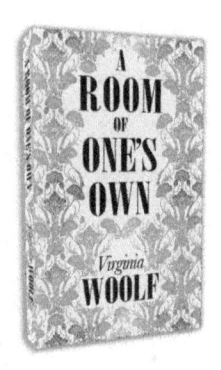

ISBN: 9781913724009
160pp • Paperback • £7.99

ISBN: 9781913724146
128pp • Paperback • £8.99

ISBN: 9781913724047
64pp • Paperback • £6.99

## DISCOVER THE FULL COLLECTION AT
WWW.RENARDPRESS.COM